SUCCESS ALCHEMY

BUILDING YOUR FUTURE | CREATING YOUR SUCCESS

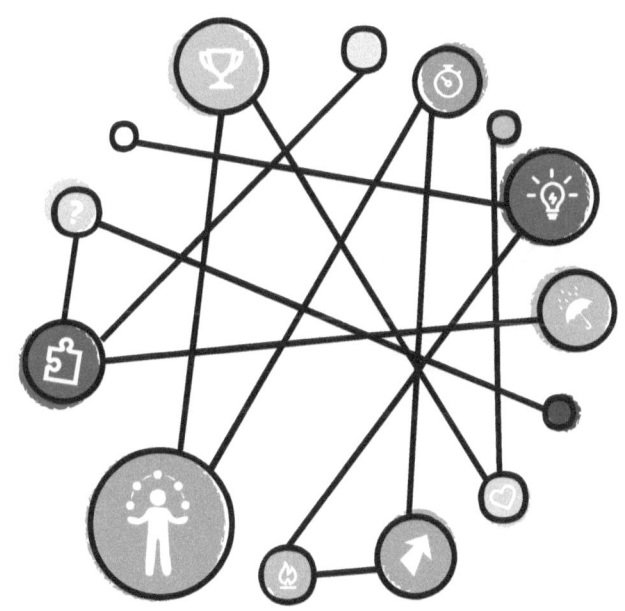

DUANE ALLEY

Copyright © 2017 by Duane Alley – http://www.DuaneAlley.com

All rights reserved. No part of this book may be produced or utilised in any form or by any means, electronic or mechanical, including photocopying, recording or by any information storage and retrieval system, without permission in writing from the publisher.

Published 2017 - Success Alchemy: Building Your Future | Creating Your Success

Publisher: Performance Results pty ltd t/as Performance Results Publishing

Graphic Design & Layout: Mélissa Caron – go-Enki.com
Editor: Richard Burian – Richard-Burian.Com

Self Help

TABLE OF CONTENTS

FORWARD 5

CHAPTER ONE: Let's Get Started 23

CHAPTER TWO: Give It Time 41

CHAPTER THREE: Find the Patterns, Find the Path 49

CHAPTER FOUR: Turning on the Flood Lights 57

CHAPTER FIVE: Digging into the Why to Find the How 73

CHAPTER SIX: Building on Failure 89

CHAPTER SEVEN: Identify the Critical Inflection Point 99

CHAPTER EIGHT: Where Did You Go? 137

CHAPTER NINE: Rewrite Your Story 151

CHAPTER TEN: Get Used to Your New Reality 151

CHAPTER ELEVEN: Time Travel 151

AFTERWORD 151

ABOUT THE AUTHOR: Duane Alley 169

FORWARD

FORWARD

You've probably heard the saying that goes, *"it's not how many times you fall down; it's how many times you get back up"* and that is just as true on the Internet and in business as it is on the playing field of life.

Can you think of a successful businessperson who has not faced some kind of failure in their career?

Probably not; because there aren't any. Behind every business success, from Oprah Winfrey to Richard Branson is a string of not-so-successful events. Oprah Winfrey got fired. Richard Branson has had spectacular failures, many of them in front of millions of people around the world. Search any of your business "models" or "heroes" and you'll find the same or similar stories. What separated these people from becoming cautionary tales was their ability to bounce back from failure.

Through this book and program I am going to share a series of 10 secrets of what I call 'Success Alchemy' that can help you turn your failures of any size and in any area of your life into successes. When I write a book, I am creating not only a good read for you (the reader); I want to allow you to immerse in a process of discovery and action. I want you to be able to take the material and apply it. Usually I refer to my books as "Doing Books" not "Just Read Me Books". So get ready for a journey of just that doing, making, and action... get ready to begin (or continue) to build your future and create the successes of your own from wherever you are in life.

This is not just a book to read and forget. The Chapters are designed to introduce the concept, give you a direction or agenda to follow and then get you moving to create real success. It's a transformative process that the most successful business people already know how to do, and I'm going to share their secrets with you.

Whether your first business failed, your latest product launch bombed, or you're on the brink of losing it all, there are lessons to be learnt and ways to recover.

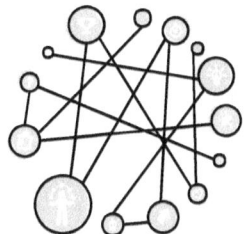

CHAPTER ONE LET'S GET STARTED

LET'S GET STARTED

Before we begin any work on "Success Alchemy" we have to cover some basic principles that you will apply throughout the journey. These principles are what I call our *Core Truths* when I'm teaching a live Training Seminar. They are purpose built to make your shifts towards success easier and your growth more powerful as well as your living of life better in all the ways you need it to be.

Usually any time you want to achieve something and are being helped, coached, mentored or guided you will be asked to set a goal or intention for the work. This is a great thing – after all – nothing gets truly achieved unless you "put it out there" that you want it.

The problem though is that so many people set their goals and then begin a cycle of stressing to get their goals... achieving their goal... and then immediately setting another bigger, better, more powerful goal to continue to "drive them forward". Think about it, what's the very next thing you do when you have achieved something? Pick something else to better it with, right?

This thinking is so common. When I ask this question in classes all over the world nearly every time 100% of the Members in the Class put their hand up and agree.

There is such a danger in doing this "natural" human process... because it's the most common thing that causes people to end up not achieving their goals and ultimately failing massively. Firstly, because there is a deep psychological imperative behind why people will continue to set bigger goals for themselves... at a deep subconscious level there is a belief that what they have just achieved isn't good enough or doesn't provide enough value or worse – they themselves aren't truly good enough and need to try to prove their worth again. It is impossible to ever truly achieve anything when we never think what we are developing, creating or doing is actually of any worth, value or benefit. We create a psychological (or thinking) cycle that is constantly reinforcing the false belief that we aren't good enough and that we don't create or even have value in our world.

The second destructive force behind constantly setting goals is the cycle we set up in our neuro-chemistry. When we create the pattern of set a goal – stress for achievement – complete and release stress – followed by immediately set and begin to stress again... this stress/release cycle sets up a cascade of chemical releases and reactions in our body that cause us stress, anxiety, aggression and ultimately overall bad emotional and physical health. We are constantly subjecting ourselves to some of the most powerful stressors our system can handle and over time we begin to associate (or in *The Science of Change*, we call it "anchor in to" the experience) this negative stress with setting and achieving goals. Subconsciously we want to avoid that stress and one of the easiest ways is to stop ourselves achieving the goal so we don't have to set and stress a new one. Think of your subconscious mind as being about a 7 to 10 year old child that loves you very much and you'll have a good idea how and why it reacts the way it does. Its job is to preserve and protect your emotional and mental state. So if something is hurting... what would a kid do? Just not do it.

Many people think of this as your mind "self-sabotaging" your results... really it's just a natural protection mechanism. And we can use our true natural mind functioning to make sure it doesn't happen. You won't need a potion, pill, process or procedure to stop this "self-sabotage" because in essence there is no such thing. There won't be a need to protect so that result disappears.

This neuro-chemical cycle can so easily be interrupted and converted into a positive by adding something very simple... a pause...

When you complete your goal – achieve the result you were after and stressing to get. Remember too, stress to achieve a goal is natural and a positive thing – it's just when you back up with another goal and stress straight away that it starts taking its toll.

When you reach the point of achievement... Rest.

Don't jump straight into another goal – do this instead...

› **Rest** – pause

› **Reward** – give yourself something as a reward for achieving your goal and make sure you at least create the thought that you are receiving this because you have achieved

› **Review** – while you are rewarding allow yourself to acknowledge the value in your achievement and your worth in having done it

Taking this path instead of the stress/release cycle allows a new cascading neuro-chemical reaction. One that brings not only a feeling of general well being but also a sense of calm and rest; powerful positive emotional states that link in the subconscious that achieving your goals creates a positive feeling. This is something the subconscious wants to experience again so will begin to partner with you to find ways to achieve your other goals so it can repeat the positive emotions... this is the exact opposite of what was happening before.

WHAT DO YOU NEED TO DO ABOUT THIS?

Two things –

For the future – begin to set your Rewards for Achievement at the same time you set your goals. Make them simple enjoyable things and not just the fact that you got what you wanted. Rather, something else you can gift to yourself and remind your self at that time you are getting this or doing this "because you achieved". Sometimes for me it's just a quiet reflection with a good coffee or my favourite tea.

For now – set yourself a Reward for achieving this book. Something you will do for or give to yourself when you have done the work ahead. Write it down in the place below and just to give you direction... if you have a date in mind when you will finish the book and the work, write a date in that you will receive your Reward.

HERE'S YOUR BIT:

WHAT IS THE REWARD?

....
....
....
....
....
....
....
....
....
....
....
....

DATE FOR REWARD?

....

NOW THAT'S DONE, IT'S TIME TO GET INTO THE DOING...
TIME TO MOVE INTO SUCCESS ALCHEMY...

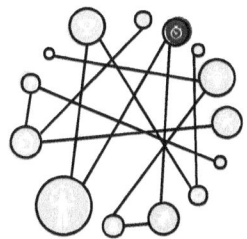

CHAPTER TWO **GIVE IT TIME**

GIVE IT TIME

In our culture of overnight successes, international "Idols", new "Voices" selected during the course of a TV season, and miraculous weight loss of hundreds of kilos in a period of weeks, it's natural that we expect to see results fast. There is so much information and forms of achievement instantly available to anyone these days. When it comes to business (and many other areas of life as well) it's oftentimes this very drive for instant success that results in our failures.

By pushing for success to occur immediately, if not sooner, we end up making choices we otherwise wouldn't have and in doing so destroying our true ability to create the success we desire.

We don't give our products time to take hold in the market before we pull the plug on them.

We don't give ourselves time to develop new habits before we decide the latest strategy (or health program, marketing campaign, sales initiative) just doesn't work.

We don't see our businesses through the tough early days and growth stages before we decide it was all a big mistake.

As a result, we let go of potential success before it has time to really take hold and grow to its full potential. Potential Success is like a seed that is buried and it needs nurturing and time to truly germinate, develop, and grow. What was a great idea is never given time to develop fully. What is a great health program (or marketing strategy) is never allowed to take hold in our habits and effect change on us. We look around at what we've planted, and not seeing enough return on our investment, we head off for greener pastures before we fully read the one we're standing in. This is what causes an entrepreneur to fill his or her shelves with the discarded boxed strategies, discs, DVDs and seminar manuals bought on a whim and dumped just as unceremoniously.

THE TRUTH IS THAT LONG-LASTING SUCCESS TAKES TIME TO DEVELOP

A strong business or a magnificent life is not created overnight. It may appear that today's blockbuster superstar came on the scene just yesterday, but what we don't see is the years of practice and rehearsals and time spent honing their craft. Likewise, we need to get our ideas, our businesses and our dreams time to develop before we decide that they're failures.

THE FAILURE JUST MIGHT BE IN YOUR MIND

Before you give up on your latest plan, ask around for input from other people. Research how long it took other companies like yours to turn a profit. Ask other people who are getting in shape how long it took them before they changed their eating and exercise habits. Read about successes in your field of interest and see what went into the development. You will probably discover that it took much longer than you had anticipated, and much longer than you've given yourself.

Just as with a seed, any business or idea or even habit has a growth process. There are stages it must go through before it can reach fruition. Skipping any one of those stages, or trying to speed them up, doesn't work.

And just like a seed and baby seedling need the sun's energy so do our new potentials need our energy. And I'm not talking about some mythic or esoteric phenomena.

When I speak of energy in this manner I mean:

ATTENTION

AWARENESS

EFFORT

With these three factors directed by us onto and into the project or goal area, it simply cannot move as fast or as far as it could and that we want. And what's critical is to allow them to "soak in". That is, to direct them long enough into the area so that they can begin to show the results. Remember many times even though you are directing your Energy into and onto a project or potential result while there are immediate underlying changes occurring, these changes won't always be evident. They need time to work outwards and upwards to be a visible tangible result you can truly see or experience. Give your work time to "blossom" or "bear fruit".

Remind yourself that success does not happen overnight, and what you see as a failure... just might be a failure of not enough time.

TAKE A GOOD LONG HARD LOOK AT YOUR CURRENT PLANS, CALENDAR AND STRATEGIES

HERE'S YOUR BIT:

WHAT'S WORKING?
Name a few methods or activities that help you reach your goals.

I succeed when I do ....
....

I succeed when I do ....
....

I succeed when I do ....
....

I succeed when I do ....
....

I succeed when I do ....
....

I succeed when I do ....
....

I succeed when I do ....
....

WHAT'S NOT?

Name a few methods or activities that don't work for you and do not help you reach your goals, even though you tried.

It doesn't help me to ....
....

It doesn't help me to ....
....

It doesn't help me to ....
....

It doesn't help me to ....
....

It doesn't help me to ....
....

It doesn't help me to ....
....

It doesn't help me to ....
....

WHAT RESULTS ARE ALREADY SHOWING? WHAT'S NOT?

✔ RESULTS SHOWING	✘ RESULTS NOT SHOWING
....	....
....	....
....	....
....	....
....	....
....	....
....	....
....	....
....	....
....	....
....	....
....	....
....	....
....	....

NOW TAKE AN EVEN MORE HONEST LOOK

Have you given this the time, awareness, attention and effort you and it deserve?

I invested my time to focus my ATTENTION on my objectives and the project:
- [ ] YES
- [ ] NOT ENOUGH
- [ ] NOT SURE

Because of this, I ....
....
....

I invested my time to reflect on the challenges of my project using my AWARENESS:
- [ ] YES
- [ ] NOT ENOUGH
- [ ] NOT SURE

Because of this, I ....
....
....

I invested my time in my project doing concrete EFFORT and actions.
- [ ] YES
- [ ] NOT ENOUGH
- [ ] NOT SURE

Because of this, I ....
....
....

CREATE HONEST TIME-LINES FOR THE NEW STRATEGIES OR EXISTING "TRIALS".

START ....

....

....

....

....

....

....

....

....

....

....

....

....

....

....

....

....

....

GOAL ....

GO BACK TO YOUR CALENDAR AND "RE-PLAN" USING YOUR NEW HONEST TIME-LINES.

Set up regular checkpoints along the way where you can truly look at results developing over time.

START ....

🚩 ....
....

🚩 ....
....

🚩 ....
....

🚩 ....
....

🚩 ....
....

🚩 ....
....

🚩 ....
....

GOAL ....

This *Agenda of Success Alchemy* is the reason I created my signature Training Series, the **Build Your Future Program** as 12- to 24-month continuing trainings rather than just a "flash in the pan" single event. The true power of change comes from ongoing staged learnings, supported growth and continual re-immersion.

Remember the strongest trees are not the ones that grow to maturity in a season. Rather they are the ones that take a lifetime. If you don't want to be a "reality show instant success and just as instant failure" then don't model them.

Go back and read this chapter again and put it to work.

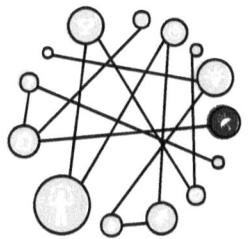

CHAPTER THREE **FIND THE PATTERNS, FIND THE PATH**

FIND THE PATTERNS, FIND THE PATH

I know that you would have heard it said many times... that... Success leaves clues. The thing is... so does failure.

It's important to review your past failures and look for those clues; discover, explore, and figure out the mystery of success. I know it seems strange in a personal development based book to ask you to look at failures and the "bad times". Generally, we're always being asked to think of the green fields, blue skies and our massive awesomeness.

So, it may seem strange to excavate your failures for keys to success, but it actually makes a lot of sense. There is an often-quoted (and probably inaccurate) phrase attributed to Thomas Edison. The numbers are usually different and the thought process and idea is the same *"he didn't fail over 1,000 times, but instead discovered over 1,000 ways something wouldn't work".*

Your own patterns of behaviour that lead to failure will lead you to success when you can discover and discern them.

When I'm working in Relationship Coaching, or Training others to do the same, some of the first questions I ask will be about the Client's past relationships, and how they failed. What were the patterns of thought, feeling and behaviour that created the result of the Relationship failing? As a good Coach I know the patterns developed and used previously often carry into the present. These patterns of thought, feeling and behaviour have developed over years and are generally so buried in the subconscious that they are not immediately recognised even by the person doing them.

Discovering those patterns, and bringing attention to them, can not only help you see where you've gone wrong before, but also help you avoid similar problems in the future.

You can do this on your own as well.

If you're trying to discover why your latest business or project failed, go back and look over all your work experiences.

› What did your past business failures have in common? For example, were they all in the same industry?

› Did they all have the same business structure?

› Were you working with the same business partner or Team?

› Did you hire similar people each time?

› Did you try to do it all yourself?

› Did you invest a lot of money, or very little?

These things may not seem to have anything in common, but they really do. Tracing patterns and similarities can help point to reasons for failure and reasons for success.

You can also do the same for life goals and projects – just look to the similar failures in the past and start to draw out the patterns that led to the failure.

So for instance – if you are having trouble maintaining relationships with friends or romantic partners... Trace where the problems are occurring.

> Do you always choose "the bad boy" or the "wrong type of girl"?

> Do you go full out at the beginning, but then put on the brakes, saying you're too busy?

> Do you smother friends and partners with attention and time, feeling insecure when they don't return your affections?

You can apply the same type of investigation and thinking to any type of personal issue or concern. The secret is to...

LOOK FOR THE PATTERNS

It may be helpful to bring in an objective set of eyes during this process. A business or personal Coach (as mentioned above) can be extremely helpful. Having someone who knows you, but who isn't intimately connected to you, can help you figure out your patterns. Not only are they trained to ask the right questions, they're also experienced enough to know many of the common pitfalls.

When you are experiencing a problem in business or life... it does not show up as an external event happening to you. Rather, it's a reality you are living now. This is what makes it so hard to "get perspective" on the problem because to you it's "just what is". And why someone from the outside can see so easily what is happening and what a better course of thinking or action would be.

You may think that you want your failures to be over and done with, never to see the light of day again. But that's short-term thinking. It's important to review what went wrong and see if you can make it go right in the future.

Once you have identified the patterns that have stopped you in the past, then it is time to also look for any powerful patterns that have helped you succeed in your own personal history as well. It is not enough to only be looking at the bad or the good. What's critical to success and achievement today is to not be doing the things that will cause you to fail and simultaneously be doing what will cause you to win.

HERE'S YOUR BIT:

WHAT IS AN AREA THAT YOU WANT TO MOVE FORWARD ON and are <u>not</u> right now?

In the future, I want to ....
....
....
....
....
....
....
....
....
....
....
....
....
....
....
....
....
....

DELVE INTO YOUR OWN PAST.

What have been some similar historical situations where you haven't achieved what you wanted?

1. I failed ....

....

....

2. I failed ....

....

....

3. I failed ....

....

....

4. I failed ....

....

....

5. I failed ....

....

....

NOW – LOOK FOR THE SIMILARITIES

in those situations of the Past and what is occurring <u>in the Present</u>.

➢ Similarities: ....
....
....

➢ Similarities: ....
....
....

➢ Similarities: ....
....
....

➢ Similarities: ....
....
....

➢ Similarities: ....
....
....

HIGHLIGHT THOSE AREAS AND PATTERNS
that have caused or led to the failure to succeed.

1. Pattern that caused failure: ....
....

2. Pattern that caused failure: ....
....

3. Pattern that caused failure: ....
....

4. Pattern that caused failure: ....
....

5. Pattern that caused failure: ....
....

6. Pattern that caused failure: ....
....

7. Pattern that caused failure: ....
....

WHAT CAN YOU DO NOW TO STOP THOSE PATTERNS
of thought, feeling or behaviour?

➤ I have to stop ....
....

➤ I have to stop ....
....

➤ I have to stop ....
....

➤ I have to stop ....
....

➤ I have to stop ....
....

➤ I have to stop ....
....

➤ I have to stop ....
....

TIME TO GO BACK TO YOUR PAST
and look for similar historical situations where you have actually succeeded.

🏆 1. I succeeded .... ___ ___ ___ ___
....

🏆 2. I succeeded .... ___ ___ ___ ___
....

🏆 3. I succeeded .... ___ ___ ___ ___
....

🏆 4. I succeeded .... ___ ___ ___ ___
....

🏆 5. I succeeded .... ___ ___ ___ ___
....

🏆 6. I succeeded .... ___ ___ ___ ___
....

🏆 7. I succeeded .... ___ ___ ___ ___
....

🏆 8. I succeeded .... ___ ___ ___ ___
....

WHAT PATTERNS OF THOUGHT, FEELING AND BEHAVIOUR
can you <u>bring forward to now</u> and begin to weave into your life or business?

- The pattern that helped me achieved this was ....
  ....

- The pattern that helped me achieved this was ....
  ....

- The pattern that helped me achieved this was ....
  ....

- The pattern that helped me achieved this was ....
  ....

- The pattern that helped me achieved this was ....
  ....

- The pattern that helped me achieved this was ....
  ....

- The pattern that helped me achieved this was ....
  ....

- The pattern that helped me achieved this was ....
  ....

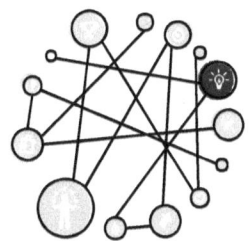

CHAPTER FOUR **TURNING ON THE FLOOD LIGHTS**

TURNING ON THE FLOOD LIGHTS

fter a failure, especially a large, or painful one... It's common to ask yourself, *"Why did this happen to me?"*

There are many people who will tell you that *"this"*... whatever *"this"* is... is part of some master plan.

Here's what I mean –

You went bankrupt? ... *"It's for the best."*

Your company went out of business? .... *"It happened for a reason."*

You suffer a broken relationship? ... *"It wasn't meant to be."*

When someone greets you with this kind of "canned" response, your desire may be to hand them some pain of their own (read this as *"smack them in the head"*).

If you believe in a higher power, it may be hard to stomach the fact that he or she (or it) would make pain a part of the "natural plan". And if you don't believe in divine purpose, you may think it's all a big lottery anyway, and you just have some bad luck.

But I ask you to look at it differently. Just for 10 seconds...

› What if there was a plan?

› What if your failure did happen for reason?

› What if 10 years from now you knew you would look back and say, *"Boy, I'm glad that happened"*?

It might be hard to go to that place where pain and failure are "meant to be". But I ask you to try, just for a moment.

Imagine that there is some huge divine (or cosmic), gorgeous plan. Imagine that everything that happens does happen for reason. Now, look at your own failure or major event, and ask what that reason might be.

› **If you went bankrupt**, can you see that your failure might help bring attention back to the real priorities in your life, or at least help get you out of the geographic area you dislike?

› **If a relationship broke up**, could it be that this will help you have the confidence to go after your own dreams?

› **Could a failed product** actually bring you to a better idea, one you wouldn't have discovered if you'd spent time and resources on your first plan?

I'm not asking you to believe that there is a higher power guiding each and every one of your movements and decisions. What I am hoping that you can see is that there is the potential for good to come out of your failure. Many times when people suffer a huge setback, whether it be battling cancer, a financial upset, or even a broken relationship, years later they often come back and say they are glad it occurred.

When my own Father died just after my 21st birthday I could not have told you of a "higher purpose" then and there. Not only had my family and I lost someone we loved deeply; in the personal and financial fallout that came with the vacuum of him not being there, we had supposed friends and family lie, steal and cheat us – we lost the family business, car, house and mental, emotional and physical health.

With nearly 2 decades past since that time I can look now at my life with gratitude for one of the most devastating events that had ever occurred to me and to my family. So much of what is now was only possible because of the growth and learning that came from "losing Dad".

IN MY TRAININGS I ASK PEOPLE TO "LOOK FOR THE LEARNINGS" AND TO <u>FORGET</u> ABOUT THE LESSONS.

I class "lessons" as what's happening in the moment. Forget them. Seek instead what is going to develop over time – the "learnings" – that will infuse your life with greater purpose and power.
You can look now with a dim candle and wait 20 years for their true importance to develop… or…

…**You can turn on the floodlights, now.** I'm trying to help you shortcut that process of waiting to see what a distant painful event might have meant. To see a glimmer of hope and turning your failure, whatever was, into a learning for the future.

HERE'S YOUR BIT:

IN YOUR PAST: WHAT ARE SOME OF THE MOST PAINFUL EVENTS you had to go through, even though you later healed from it.

1 ....
....
....

2 ....
....
....

3 ....
....
....

4 ....
....
....

5 ....
....
....

ACCORDING TO THE PREVIOUS LIST, WHAT LESSONS DID YOU LEARN in each situation and from which you benefit or make others benefit from in your present life? If you consider you didn't learn anything from a painful event, think about what you <u>want</u> to learn from it or what pattern of though you want to change that prevents you from seeing a lesson.

💡 1. This event made me ☐ LEARN ☐ WANT TO LEARN ....
....
....

💡 2. This event made me ☐ LEARN ☐ WANT TO LEARN ....
....
....

💡 3. This event made me ☐ LEARN ☐ WANT TO LEARN ....
....
....

💡 4. This event made me ☐ LEARN ☐ WANT TO LEARN ....
....
....

💡 5. This event made me ☐ LEARN ☐ WANT TO LEARN ....
....
....

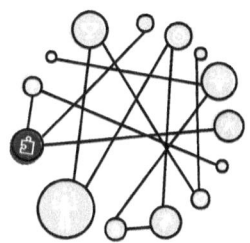

CHAPTER FIVE DIGGING INTO THE WHY TO FIND THE HOW

DIGGING INTO THE WHY TO FIND THE HOW

In a previous chapter, I asked you to review your *chain of failures* for patterns and connections. In this chapter, I want you to dive deep into your most recent failure, looking at all the little details and decision points that could have led to a negative outcome.

Businesses often conduct the *'post mortem'* of any recent project, positive or negative. They want to see what has gone right, of course, but they also want to see the points where they could have made a different decision to lead to even better results.

When conducting a project review like this there are a couple of guidelines to follow:

1. Bring together all your materials from the project

This means your scrawled notes on the back of napkins, your checklists, your spreadsheets, emails you sent to team members and customers, everything. Spread it all out in front of you in a big space and have a whiteboard handy for timelines, notes, and discoveries. You want to be able to look at everything at once, from beginning to end, without skipping anything.

 2. Don't rush it

Give yourself time to fully absorb all the different elements of your project. If this sounds intense, it is. The larger the project, the more time and energy you need to put into this process. Add more time you spend on it, the greater the returns will be.

 3. Look at specific elements

There are some common areas where decision points can go a ride. One such area is in personnel.

- ✔ Did you have the right Team?
- ✔ Did you have enough people involved?
- ✔ Did they have the right roles?

Another common area where mistakes are made is in timing.

- ✔ Did you allow yourself enough time to thoroughly plan and execute your project?
- ✔ Did things occur in the right sequence, and with the right amount of time between them?
- ✔ Finally, were you doing the right things?

Sometimes you can have all the right people and all the right timing but your project's working goal is simply wrong. It's like releasing a product to your market that it just doesn't want. It can be beautiful, you can do it right, but it still fails.

 4. Go beyond the easy answer

It's human nature to want to find one reason that something didn't work, but it's rarely that simple. There are usually a number of different factors that contributed to the success or failure of any venture. Sure, some will be big and some will be small, but there is always more than one reason – and it's rarely the one you think of first.

 5. Review your results with an objective listener

After you finish the post mortem, it's important to go over your findings with someone who knows you, knows the project, but is still an objective observer. You can present your findings to them, getting their feedback, and even reviewing some of the action items you've discovered for your next project. This outside counsel is critical to ensuring that you haven't gone for the easy answer, and that you aren't overlooking anything. A business Coach or Mentor is a great person to have involved at this stage, because they've been involved in similar processes before.

HERE'S YOUR BIT:

WHAT HAS BEEN A RECENT FAILURE?

....
....
....
....
....

With the following steps, you will work through the *5 Stage Failure Post mortem* discussed in the previous chapter.

① WHAT ARE ALL YOUR MATERIALS
from the project you will need to source and bring to this process?

....	....
....	....
....	....
....	....
....	....
....	....
....	....
....	....

DON'T RUSH IT –
schedule out the time you will need and commit to it.

....

....

LOOK AT SPECIFIC ELEMENTS

Did you have the right Team?
☐ YES   ☐ NO   ☐ NO SURE

Did you have enough people involved?
☐ YES   ☐ NO   ☐ NO SURE

Did they have the right roles?
☐ YES   ☐ NO   ☐ NO SURE

Did you allow yourself enough time to thoroughly plan and execute your project?
☐ YES   ☐ NO   ☐ NO SURE

Did things occur in the right sequence, and with the right amount of time between them?
☐ YES   ☐ NO   ☐ NO SURE

Were you doing the right things?
☐ YES   ☐ NO   ☐ NO SURE

GO BEYOND THE EASY ANSWER –
dig deeper into the causes – the *Whys*.

If you did not have the right Team, explain WHY it happened:
....
....

If you did not have enough people involved, explain WHY it happened:
....
....

If the people involved did not have the right roles, explain WHY it happened:
....
....

If you didn't allow yourself enough time to thoroughly plan and execute your project, explain WHY it happened:
....
....

If things did not occur in the right sequence, and with the right amount of time between them, explain WHY it happened:
....
....

If you were not doing the right things, explain WHY it happened:
....
....

✓5 WHO COULD BE AN OBJECTIVE LISTENER
to work through your answers?

....

....

....

USE THE "WHYS" YOU DISCOVER
AS THE INGREDIENTS FOR CREATING
THE NEW "HOWS" FOR SUCCEEDING NEXT TIME.

CHAPTER SIX **BUILDING ON FAILURE**

BUILDING ON FAILURE

In the previous chapter I wrote about reviewing or conducting a *Failure Post mortem*. This reviewing of your project and finding out where things went wrong is not the same as pointing the finger and blaming.

> **IDENTIFYING ISSUES IS CONSTRUCTIVE; BLAMING IS DESTRUCTIVE.**

Absolutely, it's natural to want to blame someone or something for your failure. We blame the holidays for a weight gain, we blame our ex for his or her lack of understanding and empathy, and we blame the market for the fact that no one bought our product.

There are several problems with this approach...

First, things are rarely that simple.

As we discovered in the last Agenda, failure can come from a number of different sources, and usually involves several different factors. Choosing just one as the "problem child" means that you can ignore other factors that could have been involved in the failure. Saying that the market is to blame for your lack of ability to sell your house ignores other elements, such as your pricing, the condition of your house, and your Real Estate Agent... any one of which can have a massive impact on the situation.

Next, blaming usually involves placing responsibility on an external person or force.

Saying that our ex was the reason our marriage failed means that we take no responsibility, and therefore have no way to impact the future. Not only is that ridiculous, it also means that nothing we do now or in the future will make things any different. We've placed ourselves firmly in the victim's role. While that means we might not have to take any responsibility, it also means that we cannot have any impact on the outcome. Since the only thing we can truly impact is our own actions, blaming others for a poor outcome means that we are giving up any possibility of things being better in the future.

**YOU MIGHT BE WONDERING WHAT THE DIFFERENCE BETWEEN IDENTIFYING PROBLEMS AND BLAMING IS...
...IT BOILS DOWN TO <u>ASSIGNING</u> FAULT...**

Maybe you think your product launch failed because the timing was all off. You chose to release a product the week after Christmas, and a half of your market was off-line. Knowing that the timing was off is identifying the issue; saying that it was Joe's fault because he chose the timing is assigning blame. It's not really important for the future to know who's fault it was; instead it's important to know how you are going to change things to improve them next time around.

It's likely that Joe already knows that he was the one who made the decision for the December launch. Pointing that out isn't going to solve anything. If he already recognizes that he was the one to make the decision, you don't need to tell him that. And if he doesn't recognise that he was the one to make the call on timing, pointing that out now isn't going to help anything either.

The best solution is simply to commit to a different decision the next time around.

You can also think of this in a personal way – blaming causes hurt feelings and wastes resources and energy. Find out where things went off track, but don't worry about whose fault it was.

HERE'S YOUR BIT:

THINK OF SITUATIONS WHERE YOU TEND TO BLAME OTHERS
and how you can resolve, avoid or improve the situation by your own actions.

👆 1. I don't take blame on ....   I can change ....

....

....

👆 2. I don't take blame on ....   I can change ....

....

....

👆 3. I don't take blame on ....   I can change ....

....

....

👆 4. I don't take blame on ....   I can change ....

....

....

👆 5. I don't take blame on ....   I can change ....

....

....

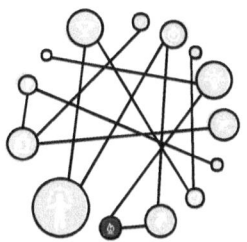

CHAPTER SEVEN IDENTIFY THE CRITICAL INFLECTION POINT

IDENTIFY THE CRITICAL INFLECTION POINT

In major disasters, it's common to be able to review what happened and point to a critical moment when things could have changed.

It's that "go/no go moment" when things could still have been salvaged, if someone had pulled the plug or chosen a different path. While there may have been a number of different decisions leading up to this moment, the project or relationship or endeavour could still have succeeded if things have taken a different turn.

In business-speak, this is sometimes called a *"critical inflection point."*

You've done a fine-toothed comb review of your failure, looking for all the multitudes of different decisions and factors that contributed to the overall failure. Right now, I'd like you to look for that one last moment when things could have turned out differently... Maybe this is a point where you decided to go ahead with the product, even though the initial response from your test audience was less than encouraging.

In a relationship, maybe it's when you chose to go on a business trip versus attending a family reunion.

If you were trying to lose weight, maybe it's when you went on the all-inclusive cruise to Alaska instead of the health spa vacation.

Before this point in time things were headed on one trajectory; afterwards, things went in a very different direction.

The reason we're looking for this point is that it's important to be able to read clues while you're in the midst of the process. You need to be able to recognise when things are changing, when the market is shifting, a relationship is moving in a different direction, or the winds are turning... for or against you.

IN THE FUTURE, YOU'RE GOING TO FACE OTHER SITUATIONS THAT CAN LEAD TO A FAILURE.

Knowing how to recognise the clues leading up to that failure is important: equally important is to know when you have an opportunity to save the project.

HERE'S YOUR BIT:

REVIEW A RECENT FAILURE:

One of my recent failure is ....

WAS THERE A CRITICAL INFLECTION POINT?

What was it/were they? Name a few moments when things could have changed the final outcome by stopping the project, by changing direction, etc.

1. Things could have changed when: ....
   ....
   ....

2. Moment when things could have changed: ....
   ....
   ....

3. Moment when things could have changed: ....
   ....
   ....

4. Moment when things could have changed: ....
   ....
   ....

5. Moment when things could have changed: ....
   ....
   ....

Hindsight is 20/20, so in retrospect, look for that moment in time when, if you just made a different choice, things would be very different now.

THERE IS NOTHING YOU CAN DO ABOUT THE OLD FAILURE NOW...
Except… Learn from it for the future. What are the learnings you can take from this to make part of your future?

- What I can learn from this is: ....
  ....
  ....

- What I can learn from this is: ....
  ....
  ....

- What I can learn from this is: ....
  ....
  ....

- What I can learn from this is: ....
  ....
  ....

- What I can learn from this is: ....
  ....
  ....

Sometimes these moments are sign-posted with all sorts of signage and clues. Your spouse tells you, *"If you go on that trip, I won't be here when you get back."* Your chief financial officer tells you, *"If you continue with the project as planned, this month's expenses will exceed revenues."* Your daughter's teacher tells her that if she fails one more test, she will have to stay back a grade.

Other times the critical inflection points aren't so easy to identify. You may have to trace back threads of decisions and timelines to see when things could have shifted. It's worth the effort to do so, as knowing how to recognize these problems can save you future failures.

No one likes to admit that failure is imminent. After all the time, energy, resources and effort that is invested into a major project, pulling the plug can be seen as a sign of defeat. But seeing the writing on the wall and not doing anything about it is an even worse decision.

Going down on the ship is bad, but seeing the iceberg ahead and not getting off when you had the chance is a true disaster.

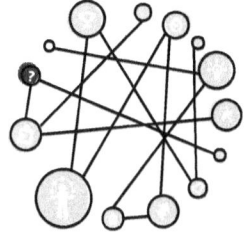

CHAPTER EIGHT **WHERE DID YOU GO?**

WHERE DID YOU GO?

Time to Plot Your Course...

You've probably heard this story before; I know I've told it in countless seminars all over the world... that between take off and landing, airplanes are off course over 90% of the time. Along the route, the job of the Pilot is not so much staying on course, but to make an ongoing series of adjustments that will bring them back in line to land at the precise point they want to.

But imagine what it would be like if they didn't make those corrections. What if they deviated a few degrees upon take off, and continued on the wrong course till the flight was over?

After all, it's just a few degrees... Right?

How big a difference could it make?

I'm sure most of us know that a few degrees' change over time can result in a huge deviation at the endpoint.

The longer the flight, the greater the deviation.

Let's transfer this analogy to your business and success...

Get off track at the beginning of your project (without correction), and you may never recover. Meanwhile if you're nearly there, a few wrong turns won't do much damage.

Review your failure through this lens. Consider the critical inflection points we identified in the previous article.

› At what point in the trajectory of your project do they occur?

› Are they at take off, landing, or somewhere in the middle?

› And when you got off course, which direction did you head?

Maybe you were brought to a standstill, dead in the water. Maybe you actually went backwards. Maybe you got pulled to one side or another, distracted by another project or issue.

After you know which direction you went, the next logical question is why you strayed. What was it that grabbed your attention? Was it an emergency in another area of your business or project, or an (alternative, seemingly more) attractive project that promised more return on investment? Or maybe you got scared and stopped the project, or took a few steps backward, convinced that you need more research or information before you could move ahead.

Identifying where you went off track and why are great pieces of information as you move forward into other projects.

The past is the past – remember Failure at any point is just that, a point in time. If we carry it with us as a belief about ourselves it becomes a personality. It is at that point we're in serious trouble...

Use this review of your previous project or business failures to uncover the learning to move forward with. You can then carry the learnings forward and not the moment of failing.

HERE'S YOUR BIT:

TAKE A PAST EVENT, PROJECT OR BUSINESS FAILING

One of my failure is ....
....
....
....
....
....
....
....
....
....
....
....
....
....
....
....
....
....
....
....
....

PLOT ITS COURSE...

Look for the critical inflection points (the points of choice or decision that changed everything.)

1. Important decision in that situation: ....
....
....

2. Important decision in that situation: ....
....
....

3. Important decision in that situation: ....
....
....

4. Important decision in that situation: ....
....
....

5. Important decision in that situation: ....
....
....

AT WHAT POINT IN THE TRAJECTORY OF YOUR PROJECT DO THEY OCCUR?
Are they at take off, landing, or somewhere in the middle?

The trajectory changed at the Critical Inflection Point # ....

AND WHEN YOU GOT OFF COURSE, WHICH DIRECTION DID YOU HEAD?

BACKWARD	STANDSTILL	FORWARD
☐	☐	☐

WHY DID YOU GO OFF COURSE AT THAT POINT?
Look for the reason or distraction that took you in that direction.

....
....
....
....
....
....
....
....
....
....

WHY DID THAT OCCUR AT THAT TIME?

....
....
....
....
....
....
....
....
....

WHY DID THAT HAPPEN WHEN IT DID?

....
....
....
....
....
....
....
....
....
....

DRILL DOWN...

...Until you have your learning able to be taken through to your next (or maybe even current) project.

When you are plotting your course from previous events, projects, etc. and preparing your new adventure, you are looking back at the patterns of thought, feeling and behaviour. You are reviewing what has been. It is sometimes very easy to get caught up in the past and live it like the present. When this happens, we are allowing ourselves to fall into the shame of failure or the blame of *"whose fault"*.

Simple solution – Don't! Realise you are only reviewing in order to find the pattern and then dig into it for the learning. Where you went off course and why it happened at that time with the express purpose of learning to not allow that to happen again. There is no benefit in taking a "head in the sand" approach to the future… it does not help to say that you are going to completely forget about your past and focus only on where you want to go.

This is a *Personal Development Delusion* that will keep you trapped in the same patterns forever. It is critical that we uncover, understand and undo the limiting patterns of thought, feeling and behaviour that caused the failure in the past so that we can create new powerful patterns that will bring about our success and achievement.

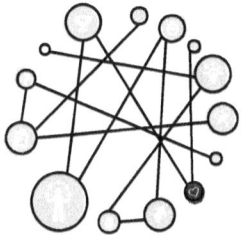

CHAPTER NINE **REWRITE YOUR STORY**

REWRITE YOUR STORY

One of the hardest parts of failure is having a black mark on your personal history. People who have gone through a business failure, bankruptcy, or divorce often express feelings of depression. Suddenly, their vision of themselves has completely changed. Instead of being the winner of their own story, they've become a loser. And no one wants to be a loser.

The solution: Rewrite your story.

Therapists use this with children who have experienced abuse. They are asked to reframe (this means, change the meaning of) their history of abuse and see themselves as a survivor rather than a victim. This shift of perspective isn't just an exercise in storytelling; it can radically change one's view on the events in his or her life, as well as the outlook for the future. This change from "victim" to "survivor" isn't just a replacement of a label; it becomes a lens through which life, history, future and reality are viewed. In Jungian psychology we'd call this an archetype. We use the same process when working with *Symbolic Coaching Methods*.

Here's how you can apply this to your life:

Let's say you were let go from your dream job in the recent recession. You have had trouble finding work, and had to take a position far below your capabilities, delivering pizza at night to make ends meet. You might be thinking, *"I'm such a loser, I can't even get another job."*

STOP!

Rewrite your story in a positive manner. Instead of being a loser, you're not willing to take unemployment or be supported by family members till you get a job you consider at "your level." You'll do what you have to, to support yourself. Look at the characteristics you're exhibiting: Perseverance, pride, and a strong work ethic – all far from "loser-hood".

Here's another example. You planned your first webinar and had three attendees, with your expenses far outpacing your revenue. You feel like a complete failure, and you're ready to throw in the towel completely.

Let's rewrite this event: You haven't lost anything. Instead, you've learned some important skills and lessons. You've taken a risk, and while it didn't turn out the way you'd planned, one mistake does not make a business failure. Instead of thinking it's a message you should quit, see at as the necessary "first draft" of your story.

HERE'S YOUR BIT:

GO BACK AND REVIEW A PREVIOUS EVENT, SITUATION OR FAILURE THAT YOU ARE STILL CARRYING THE NEGATIVE EMOTIONS AND THOUGHTS.

These are patterns of feeling and thought that will direct your behaviour in the future. It's critical to uncover them.

Give yourself about 15 minutes to "story-tell" the event – write it out like a story. Keep it in third person – that is like you were the narrator and not the central character.

Use words like "he / she" rather than "I / me".

As you start to write the story keep looking for the linkages you have made that make no sense – because this happened, then the character thought they were stupid, etc.

Get it all out though – all the embarrassment the character might have felt; all the blame they might have had for themselves or others. Get really clear on what your current "story" is you've been carrying around.

This is the actual Life Story of .... ------>

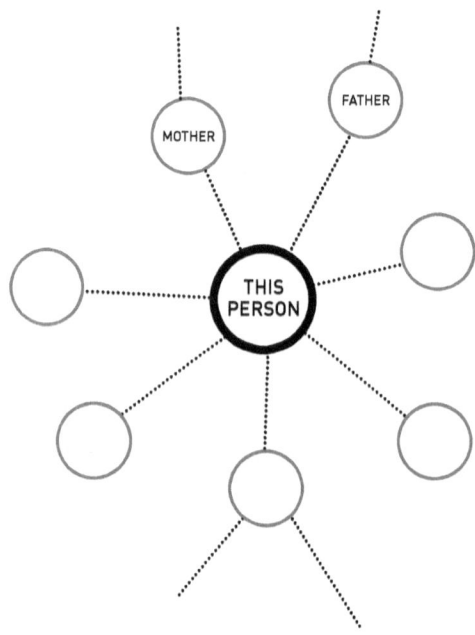

CHAPTER NINE: REWRITE YOUR STORY

NOW

Tear that story out put it in an envelope – you never have to look at this story again.

BEGIN TO RE-WRITE THE STORY.

This time tell the story in first person – that is as you being the main character using the word "I" etc. Shift the meanings and your perspective as described in the examples above. Find the meaning and reason as well as the learning for the future from that past seeming "failure". Look for those learnings that will build your patterns of empowerment and achievement in the now and into the future.

You may wish to play positive and uplifting music while you re-write this story. Keep yourself to between 15 – 20 minutes to "re-write".

....
....
....
....
....
....
....
....
....
....
....
....

When you are done – read back through your story aloud. Allow any positive emotions to come up and begin to recognise how you can use the same learnings today and tomorrow.

When you have finished reading the *New Story* (True Story) – tear up the old story sealed in the envelope or if it's safe to do so ceremoniously burn it (without opening the envelope).

If it's up to us to decide how we want to tell our stories, why not choose a positive spin on it? Claiming how you define yourself is the first step.

The next chapter is all about your next step.

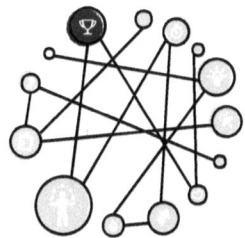

CHAPTER TEN **GET USED TO YOUR NEW REALITY**

GET USED TO YOUR NEW REALITY

In Chapter 9, we talked about redefining your story, and how doing so can provide you the strength and hope to move forward. Now, I'd like to challenge you to accept your failures as part of your past.

As much as you'd like to cut them out or pretend they never happened, they are part of you. Refusing to accept it, ignoring it, or trying to mask the past are all sure ways to make the burden heavier to carry.

When you hate a part of yourself – whether your relationship failures, your lack of physical health, or financial issues – that maps over into other areas. It's hard to feel good about work if you're still beating yourself up for the failure of your marriage or last relationship. It's equally hard to appreciate your great family life if you hate yourself for how much you weigh. As much as you try, you can't compartmentalise your life; it's all a part of a whole.

The solution is to work on accepting yourself and your new reality.

If you had to downgrade your lifestyle, stop hating on your ten-year-old family car that took the place of your BMW. Treat your new, smaller home with respect and love. Embrace where you are now, as much as you might wish to be somewhere else.

You can still have goals and dreams. I'm definitely not saying that you have to give those up; instead, keep them, love them and focus on their achievement as well.

I am saying it's critical that you accept the past as it occurred. Once you've reframed it, find opportunities to tell that story to others. Just as those in recovery programs such as AA use their stories to inspire others, you too can use your history to help. When you do so, you'll start to find the hidden gems inside your "failures".

Please be careful: It can be tempting to look around you and be convinced that no one else has failed like you have, or is suffering like you are. STOP IT – that's an easy lie to tell your self and it's just that – a lie.

Sometimes the most successful people hide the biggest scars. Name any famous person, from Abraham Lincoln to Bill Gates, and underneath the outward success lays a string of very human failures. (You need look no further than the cover of "People" magazine to see that wealth and physical beauty don't ensure happiness or marital success.)

While I don't know the details of the failures you've experienced, I do know this: Telling your true story (the re-written, positive one) to others won't just help you, it'll help them, too.

The limiting patterns of thought, feeling and behaviour that you have uncovered in yourself and have replaced with powerful positive patterns will be more evident in the people around you. And people you talk to will recognise elements of their own "story" in that which you are telling. Simply by listening to you and your story told positively, they will begin to shift their own perspective on their life. Make sure you've gone back and done the work from Chapter 9 though – it's critical that you are telling the powerful story and not the old painful one.

HERE'S YOUR BIT:

YOUR CHALLENGE: ACCEPTING FAILURES FROM THE PAST.
Look at your New Story on page 101 and note down the failures that are still hard to accept or to talk about for you. What parts of your story sound *Painful* rather than *Powerful*?

1. I find it hard to accept or talk about ....
   ....

2. I find it hard to accept or talk about ....
   ....

3. I find it hard to accept or talk about ....
   ....

4. I find it hard to accept or talk about ....
   ....

5. I find it hard to accept or talk about ....
   ....

6. I find it hard to accept or talk about ....
   ....

FROM PAINFUL TO POWERFUL.

Look at the list on the previous page and take a few minutes to think how your can re-write the Painful memories into Powerful ones. Use he" or "she" in order to let you analyze the Painful memories from a distant perspective and give the yourself empathy you deserve.

💔 **1.** In this situation, this person suffered because of ....

....

....

....

🏆 and overcame ....

....

....

....

....

💔 **2.** This person suffered because of ....

....

....

....

🏆 and overcame ....

....

....

....

....

3. This person suffered because of ....
....
....
....

and overcame ....
....
....
....
....

4. This person suffered because of ....
....
....
....

and overcame ....
....
....
....
....

5. This person suffered because of ....

....
....
....

and overcame ....

....
....
....
....

6. This person suffered because of ....

....
....
....

and overcame ....

....
....
....
....

Look back at your New Story on the page 101 and review it. Replace the Painful memories with the Powerful ones. Read this story again when you struggle with Painful memories to remind yourself of the Powerful version of your own new Life Story.

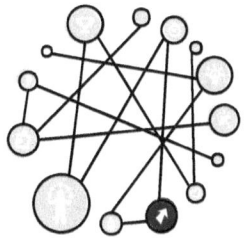

CHAPTER ELEVEN **TIME TRAVEL**

TIME TRAVEL

Once you work through all the recommended steps, you may think your job is done. You've reviewed, reframed, accepted and analysed. Now it's time to just move on, right?

Well, sort of. You've done a lot of hard work to turn your not-so-successful events into positive experiences, and you deserve kudos for that.

> **YOUR JOB ISN'T QUITE OVER.**
> **DON'T CLOSE THAT BOOK YET**

Any person of experience will tell you that the true lessons from their past didn't reveal themselves for some time, in some cases, a decade or more. It wasn't till years later that the businessman realises the early failures in his sales career taught him perseverance and determination, skills that would be called into play as he led a multi-million-dollar company through tough times.

The Mum of three didn't realise till her kids were grown and gone that the lessons she learned about juggling personal and professional responsibilities would serve her as she works with single mothers in an outplacement agency.

The football player who got injured in the first game of the season didn't realise at the time that he'd need to call on that same skill of resilience when he worked in his career as a sports agent and helped others through a similar situation.

That's why it's up to you to continue to revisit these parts of your past, continuing to look for patterns and clues that may only reveal themselves in time. That's not to say you have to go through the same level of dissection. But it is important to periodically review your downfalls.

A good time to do this exercise for your business is part of your annual planning, either with your Business Coach or on your own. When you sit down to look at what your plan is for the future, take a look back as well. Look for the same things: *Patterns, clues, and learnings*. Then use that information in your planning.

For more personal topics, you can conduct this review with a trusted friend or your own Personal Coach.

In either case, you may want to keep a log – a section in your notebook, or a file on your computer – where you keep your associated notes.

While you may think it's not worth the effort to revisit the past, it's a step in the process you shouldn't skip if you truly want to continue to turn once-thought failure into true and continuing success. You never know what lessons you may learn for the future by taking the time to go back.

AFTERWORD

AFTERWORD

Failure is, simply put, a fact of life. While we cannot avoid it completely, we can choose how we react to it, and whether we use it to inform our future. There are learnings hidden in each of our life experiences. It's up to us to decide if we're going to go through the – sometimes admittedly painful – excavation process.

I hope *Success Alchemy* has provided you some suggestions for how you can transform your own tough experiences into the foundations for future success.

Remember, you're never alone in this process. If you feel you need support – and we all do – you have many resources online and off. Trusted friends and family members will always be there to help create a shift in perspective for you. Many times though, they are part of the same patterns that brought you to the failure in the first place or at least they might have a very similar outlook or world-view as you. Speaking to someone "outside your world" is incredibly important when you truly want to shift and change. Seek great Coaches and Mentors – in business and life and recognise the changes <u>and</u> greatness you are creating.

ABOUT THE AUTHOR
DUANE ALLEY

TRAINER | AUTHOR | SPEAKER | COACH

Duane Alley spent the first 15 years of his professional life working with some of the biggest and fastest growing retail and franchise businesses in the country; he then spent 5 years as Head Trainer & Coach for one of the biggest Personal Development companies on the planet.

He has combined his extensive experience from the business world in delivering real world results with his success and study of personal development, rapid human change and shifting consciousness.

As a Master Trainer, Author, Speaker and Performance Coach he now works with businesses and entrepreneurs quickly and easily improve their businesses and make more money and with individuals, couples and families to make simple changes and take small steps to live better lives day by day.

KEEP IN TOUCH:

- DUANEALLEY.COM
- FACEBOOK.COM/DUANEALLEYPAGE
- TWITTER.COM/DUANEALLEY
- YOUTUBE.COM/DUANEALLEY
- SUCCESS@DUANEALLEY.COM

FIND OUT
the BASIC HABITS THAT WINNERS USE ON A DAILY BASIS to CONSTANTLY IMPROVE THEIR LIVES!

In the latest in the *Seven Secrets series*, Duane Alley shows you seven habits that will get you connected with your goals, help you to keep focus on them, stay on the track to your target and resist every obstacle that tries to knock you off the path. The book also takes you through a number of interactive exercises that will help you to fine-tune the details and prepare you for the road to success.

Read this book and get the tools to live your LIFE to its FULLEST!

WHAT YOU WILL LEARN:

- ☑ Focussing solidly on your outcome
- ☑ Taking immediate strategic action
- ☑ Being fully aware and attentive
- ☑ An unstoppable ability to adapt
- ☑ Decision making super-powers

Join Master Trainer, Duane Alley, in his latest book and find out how you can immediately gain focus and take action from the minute you are awake to the time you are asleep. Soon, you will be on the path to achieving your goals, dreams and greatest desires.

VISIT DUANE ALLEY TRAINING ONLINE STORE:
WWW.DUANEALLEY.COM

Discover the
7 simple secrets
of how to have abundant energy in your day to day life so you can take on the world and have everything
you deserve!

Have you ever wondered how some people just seem to overflow with energy and enthusiasm? Have you met people who always seem to be naturally "up" and "switched on" all the time, no matter how hard they play? Have you ever wanted to enjoy a level of energy that would allow you to do what you need to in life... and have ample left "in the tank" to do **EVERYTHING you WANT** as well?

Master Trainer, Duane Alley, is back with the second book in the *7 Secrets Series*. Discover the secrets to having incredible amounts of energy every day so you can truly create the life of your dreams and be able to enjoy it with those you love.

VISIT DUANE ALLEY TRAINING ONLINE STORE:
WWW.DUANEALLEY.COM

Discover
the simple secrets and small steps that together create **a new way** of **living better** day by day!

Most people focus so intently on the achievement of a goal or goals. What they forget or have never been taught is that the achievement of a goal is a fixed point in time. It is a single event that happens and once done is over.

What we truly desire to be focussed on is the creation of the life we want after we have achieved the goal. After all, the reason we achieved the goal was to have the life we get afterwards — make sense?

We get so hung up on "achievement" as the ultimate aim that we forego the real reward which is living an incredible life as we design it or choose it to be.

Join Master Trainer, Duane Alley, for 7 Minutes a Day and uncover a brand new way of focus and action so you can wake up every morning and plan every week to guarantee you are on path to achieving your goals, dreams and greatest desires.

VISIT DUANE ALLEY TRAINING ONLINE STORE:
WWW.DUANEALLEY.COM

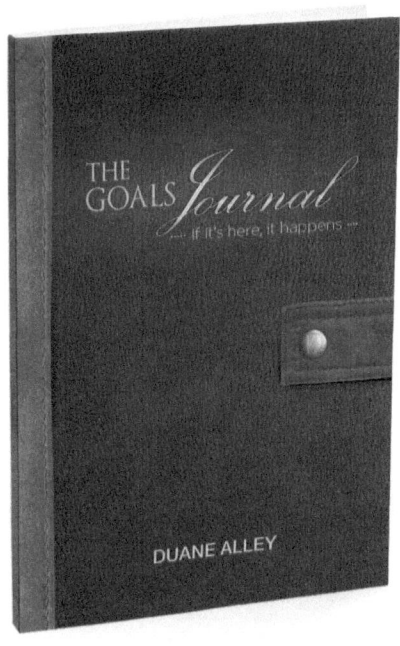

THE GOALS JOURNAL

PAPERBACK JOURNAL BOOK

Learn and use the power **Goals Journal** Process from Master Trainer & Coach, Duane Alley.

This Journal is perfect and allows for up to 100 Goals to be detailed in the amazing process combining *Science of Change*, positive psychology tools and targeted visualisation to ensure that every one of your goals details and described in this Journal happen.

Based on years of research, development and modeling of some of the greatest achievers of our time, this book is a must for anyone serious about getting results.

VISIT DUANE ALLEY TRAINING ONLINE STORE:
WWW.DUANEALLEY.COM

GIFT OF GRATITUDE JOURNEY

PAPERBACK JOURNAL BOOK

The Gift of Gratitude is a one of the Powerful "Inner Games of Excellence" discussed in Duane Alley's Best Selling book *7 Secret Habits of Success*.

This book is a 6 month Journey to truly understanding and appreciating the incredible power of "Gratitude" in our lives.

As a structured journal and easy to follow and allow system of bringing Gratitude into our lives everyday, this book changes your live, love, living and ultimately the success you create around you everyday.

VISIT DUANE ALLEY TRAINING ONLINE STORE:
WWW.DUANEALLEY.COM

MAKE IT SIMPLE BOOK

PAPERBACK BOOK

Around the world, millions of people struggle with stress, anxiety, or mood problems. These issues can wear and tear on your body and mind leaving you feeling tired, drained, and empty inside. Over time, stress and anxiety can build causing you to be less productive, anxious, tense, and very unhappy.

Is it possible to exist without stress? NO!

But stress, in and of itself, isn't bad. Confronting stress is a science and an art. If you prefer to live a happy and productive life, you have to learn how to more effectively deal with it.

Accompany me on this energising journey, which can bring a modification in your life, and determine how you too can make your life (negative-) stress free or with significantly less (bad-)stress.

VISIT DUANE ALLEY TRAINING ONLINE STORE:
WWW.DUANEALLEY.COM

HOW TO STOP BURNOUT BOOK

PAPERBACK BOOK

SIMPLE STEPS TO SURVIVE THE STRESSFUL SITUATIONS OF EVERYDAY LIFE.

Learn how to notice and fight the signs of burnout and the blues even before they take hold!

Get a copy of the book for yourself or a friend in need of guidance!

VISIT DUANE ALLEY TRAINING ONLINE STORE:
WWW.DUANEALLEY.COM

BUSINESS BREAKTHROUGH BASICS BOOK

PAPERBACK BOOK

BACK TO SCHOOL LESSONS FOR BUSINESS SUCCESS AT ANY LEVEL!

I wrote this book to help you get your "stuff" together as a business person. When I'm working with many business people either in my live trainings or private coaching/consulting, the number of people who have missed the basics constantly surprises me. They've got all the fancy strategies and do-dads but the fundamentals are absent. It's like a school student returning to school without any books at all.

So take the time now to commit to sitting down and not only reading this book – but learning from it and readying yourself to put the lessons to work or your business.

VISIT DUANE ALLEY TRAINING ONLINE STORE:
WWW.DUANEALLEY.COM

NOTES

NOTES

www.ingramcontent.com/pod-product-compliance
Lightning Source LLC
Chambersburg PA
CBHW030445300426
44112CB00009B/1171